It Takes a Village to Raise the Bar: A New Paradigm for Black America

Dr. Boyce Watkins

Boyce Watkins

Printed in the United States of America

First Printing, 2015

Ordering Information:

Special discounts are available on quantity purchases by corporations, associations, and others.
For details, contact the store@yourblackworld.net.

Orders by U.S. trade bookstores and wholesalers. Please contact the Your Black World Store by
visiting www.store.yourblackworld.com or emailing store@yourblackworld.net.

ISBN-13: 978-1508495208
ISBN-10: 1508495203

I do not consider myself to be an extraordinary man. I am not anybody's hero. I sometimes even wonder if I'm really all that smart. But one of the things that I can tell you right now is that I am determined. I am absolutely, unconditionally determined to ensure that the future of my community is better than the past. I believe that my role as a black intellectual is to make the world a better place than it was on the day that I arrived on this planet.

Sometimes, battles like this can be lonely, since it seems that there are too many in our community who either don't care, or don't feel empowered enough to be able to get anything done. But I'm not talking to those people right now. I'm talking to those who care about making their community strong, vibrant and capable as we push forward into the 21st century.

To be honest, I believe that too many scholars feel that our role should be minimal or that our job is to do what's best for ourselves and not think about anybody else. I do not agree with this assessment. I've founded websites like FinancialJuneteenth.com because I was tired of being a slave. I was tired of feeling like someone else always controlled my destiny. I would think about the runaway slaves on the plantation 300 years ago and how many of them escaped because they were living lives that they didn't want to live.

These slaves watched their loved ones get raped, beaten, tortured, castrated and mistreated, and there was nothing they could do about it. They saw their families being ripped apart. They saw their futures being controlled by other people.

Even the right to learn how to read was taken away from most of our ancestors. But in the midst of those very dark times, even when freedom seemed to be impossible, there was always that slave who dreamed of a better day.

There was always that person on the plantation who said, "Maybe we're supposed to live better than this. In fact, maybe we should fight against this system that is designed to oppress us."

Many of us like to fantasize about and identify with the runaway slave, believing that we would have fought "massa" from the minute we arrived on the slave ship. We also like to think that we would have supported the runaway slave and maybe even run away ourselves.

Let's be real. Nobody wanted to hang around with the runaway slave. The runaway slave likely had few friends on the plantation. Many people thought the runaway slave was crazy and at the very least, was going to get them all into trouble. Even those who supported the runaway slave only did so in private, due to their fear of what would happen if "massa" ever found out what they were up to.

The same thing is true for many of us on our jobs when we decide to take a stand against blatant oppression. Most people are too afraid or too financially insecure to take a stand with you. Instead, they'd rather stand behind you or only stand with you in private. This fear is natural. Oppression has a huge psychological impact on those who are affected.

What is also true, unfortunately, is that the first runaway slave probably got caught when he tried to leave the plantation. We can't over-romanticize things and pretend that he didn't get beaten, killed, castrated, humiliated, hanged or had his/her foot cut off for defying the master's enslavement. There was a lot of money on the line for slave masters, so their primary objective in life was to crush the soul and mind of the slave so badly, he would never even think about crossing the master.

Let's not pretend that if we had lived during slavery, all of us would want to be the runaway slave, because that's just a bold-faced lie. The fact is that the runaway slaves, the individuals who wanted freedom and were willing to fight for it or perhaps even die for it, were typically in the minority. Also, many of those individuals were not successful in their goal of leaving the plantation.

As I mentioned earlier, the first runaway slave probably didn't get away. He was dragged back to the plantation, beaten within an inch of his life, humiliated beyond recognition, and sometimes even killed. In the midst of all the torture, pain and tragic consequences for having the audacity to want something better, there was always that Negro standing over top of the runaway slave, saying, "N*gger, I told you so."

Most of us who dare defy and speak up against white supremacy are also confronted with the same black people, those who claim they want to "help" us by telling us to tone it down or not be so radical, even when our people are being killed by the impact of racial oppression. Much of this attitude is rooted in the experience on the plantation, where the punishment for deviation was tremendous, and no one would dare stand up against the master.

But understand this, the runaway slave, even though he probably failed in his goal of obtaining freedom, was the first visionary on the plantation. He planted a seed of inspiration and freedom that led to the next generation believing that there was a more desirable possibility, a better reality meant for black people and their children. He was the one who would inspire the next slave to try to escape from the plantation against all odds and maybe try a different route, pick a different strategy, or figure out a different way to get the freedom that was denied of his ancestors.

And HE was often a SHE.

The first runaway slave was the person who instilled the hunger and desire for freedom in our people that eventually led to the creation of the Underground Railroad. He was the first person who taught the other slaves that this system is wrong. Even if he died, even if he didn't succeed, even if he was ridiculed, the first runaway slave was the most important freedom fighter on the plantation, but not because he was successful at everything he did. Instead, the first runaway slave mattered because he planted visionary seeds of motivation that would grow into trees of freedom.

The first runaway slave opened the door for future slaves to dream bigger, try harder, and figure out solutions to previously unsolvable problems. He made the impossible possible and realities were born that were previously inconceivable. He was the originator of all that we would ever come to be in America, the alpha which brought our omega into existence.

In fact, I dare say that you can't have the first black president without the first runaway slave.

When I write these words, I am talking to my fellow runaway slaves, not those who are afraid of the master. I'm talking to other black people who are looking around in their community and are sick and tired of some of the things they're seeing.

We are sick and tired of black people being treated as second-class citizens.

We are sick and tired of our children being left uneducated.

We are sick and tired of seeing our babies shot dead in the street.

We are sick and tired of black people not advancing.

We are sick and tired of the world believing that we are somehow inferior to other people, when the fact is that we are capable of being the greatest people on the planet.

We are sick and tired of the toxic music being thrust onto our children by major radio stations, making them think that they are meant to be nothing but hoochies, ballers, rappers, thugs, killers and other things that are going to put them in an early grave.

We're sick of seeing black people going to prison.

We're sick and tired of other people controlling our destiny,

We are action-oriented and looking for a way out of the mess we see all around us. Our destiny should belong to us and nobody else, but the media controls our minds as if we have a puppet master's hand in our rear end. When I write these words, I'm talking to people who can go there with me, who can see a vision that is greater and more meaningful than the here and now.

To be honest, this message is not for the masses. I'm talking to the true black elite.

I'm not talking about the intellectually elite. I'm not talking about the economically elite. I am talking about the SPIRITUAL elite.

The spiritual elite consists of individuals who are deeply committed to seeing our community get to a place that we've never been before. I'm referring to those who can commit themselves to proactively constructing a vision of something that doesn't yet exist today. This is a multi-generational vision, one that is meant for our grandchildren's grandchildren.

I'm going to talk about the new paradigm.

The New Paradigm for Black America is an initiative that we began last year. When I created YourBlackWorld.net a few years ago, one of the things that we desperately wanted to do was help to structure a new paradigm of thought for black leaders of the 21st century.

Our goal was to use what I've learned in my 20 years of teaching on college campuses to help us to construct new dimensions of thought as it pertains to four key areas: wealth, education, family and community.

The fact is that many of us just have it wrong. We value the wrong things, we teach our children in the wrong way, we respond to racism in ways that are clearly counter-productive. Many of us are trained to start digging our own graves from the day we leave our mother's womb, and this cannot continue.

When it comes to wealth, we love to give our money away to the same people who refuse to give us jobs. We spend our money on things that make us feel good instead of things that will brighten our future. We would rather work for other people and have them pay our bills than to learn to pay our bills with our own resources.

America is being left behind academically, and black America is falling behind even further than that. Many of our children are taught to forgo educational opportunities for bogus phantom jobs in sports and entertainment. Some of us even believe that being intelligent is "acting white." For some (not all) of us, the word "excellence" only enters into our vocabulary when it comes to playing a sport or entertaining white folks.

Of course we know that many of our families have fallen apart. Black Americans were hit especially hard due to the War on Drugs and Mass Incarceration. Now, some people feel fathers are no longer mandatory. As a result, children aren't raised with the kind of family structure that provides them with the self-esteem to form productive relationships into adulthood. In other countries, the family is the center of the wealth-building exercise, so by improperly constructing our families, we are creating numerous problems in almost every other relevant arena.

Community is the nexus of wealth, education and family. If you are financially destitute, uneducated and have poorly-structured families, then it is extremely difficult to form a strong and vibrant community. The mother must be there for the son. The father must be there for his wife. The daughter must be able to depend on her uncle. The lost child must be able to depend on a neighbor for help, support or protection in case his parents are not around.

Much of this has been lost, but not entirely.

The future can be reclaimed, but it is going to have to start with us loving ourselves enough to STOP listening to other people. We can't keep begging, seeking approval or getting into meaningless spats with those who will never want to see black people prosper. As I said, it is going to require a new paradigm of thought.

Why I wrote this book

The objective of this book is to serve a few purposes, all of which are communicated in the title.

First, I believe that one important dimension in our quest for advancement as a community is that we must reclaim the village. The village isn't just for raising children, it is also for raising our awareness, raising our income levels, and raising our state of existence.

In other words, the village relates to raising the bar.

The village is what reminds us that we're all connected, and that the failure of a few of us can be connected to the failure of all of us. You can't just look at the drug addict down the street and think that it won't eventually affect you, because it eventually will.

The concerned parent who hears record labels and media conglomerates marketing black self-destruction can't simply say, "Well, it's up to the parents to monitor what their kids listen to." The fact is that if another child down the street hasn't been raised or loved properly, then his violent behavior may end up taking the life of your child.

We can no longer look at celebrities who aren't giving back to their people and conclude that it's not their responsibility to support the community that has given so much to them. The fact is that to whom much is given, much is required. You can't do Facebook posts bragging about how much money you have while ignoring calls to donate or support important projects in your own community.

Can you imagine how much stronger our Historically Black Colleges and Universities (HBCUs) would be if every black celebrity committed just 1% of their income to supporting the education of black youth? The amount they would be expected to contribute wouldn't be any greater than what they might already spend on cars they don't need, 10 vacations a year, or "popping bottles" at a strip club.

It is expected that all of us be a part of the village and support it. If you're choosing not to be a part of the village, that's OK. Just don't expect the village to support you when your oppressors have left you hanging out to dry.

We must consistently raise the bar as a community, but also as individuals. We must re-commit ourselves to excellence, and our children as well. We can no longer accept a world where athletic superiority is expected, while educational inferiority has become the norm.

We live in the information age, where anyone can become an expert on anything, at any time. You no longer have to go to school in order to get a good education. You don't have to have money in order to learn. You can get a Virtual PhD on your cell phone by reading Wikipedia pages on topics that interest you. There are YouTube videos that can help you become an expert in science, math, chemistry, business, music or any other topic you find interesting.

The world is your oyster if you are willing to open your mind and consume it. Gone are the days when you needed a white man's permission to learn at the highest levels. Now, if you don't understand how to do something or are missing the knowledge you need, you can only blame the person who lives in your mirror.

Raising the bar also means pushing our children to be the best they can be in every aspect of life. Recently, I spoke to a young mother who had a daughter that was making straight As in school. The girl was just a freshman in high school, and I asked, "Did you think about letting her take college classes?"

She was surprised to hear me make that suggestion. But I then told her the story about the parents of Dr. David Van Valen, who pushed their sons to do high school work at the age of 8. When the school district wouldn't let her sons into high school, Mrs. Van Valen and her husband homeschooled their sons for three years and sent them to high school at 11. As if that weren't impressive enough, they then had the boys take college classes for the next three years so they could go to MIT at the age of 14.

The standards you set for your children are going to dictate how they choose to live their lives. (If you listen to any highly-accomplished black man, he will typically tell stories about how his mother inspired him to be the best he could be.) He might talk to you about how his father taught him to be strong. These are the same lessons you should be giving to your children, because what you say to them is the gospel.

We also want to raise the bar when it comes to our families and keeping them together. Although mistakes do happen, children are not meant to be raised without fathers. A single parent household should be the result of an unexpected, unpreventable outcome, and not a repetitive, predictable occurrence that happens over and over due to poor planning and a lack of discipline. Fathers must fight to remain in the lives of their children, even if that means going to court. Mothers must respect the role of the father in their children's lives and take the time to choose good men to sleep with. We can't go through life being guided by our genitalia and must respect the power of reproduction.

About the New Paradigm for Black America

You don't have to be on television to be a black leader. If you have children in your home, then you are a black leader. If you have people in your space who are under your influence, then you are a black leader. If you have a desire for a better future for your community, then you are a black leader, even if you have to start by leading yourself.

As a reminder, the four key components of the New Paradigm are wealth, education, family and community. These are the four fundamental building blocks for the resurrection of black America so that we might see ourselves as the great men and women we are meant to become.

In 2013, we conducted a series of forums around the country based on the New Paradigm. The first one was in Chicago with Minister Louis Farrakhan from the Nation of Islam.

Minister Farrakhan is, in my opinion, one of the greatest black men in American history. Whether you like him or not, you have to realize that he has the ability to do something that most of us cannot do, which is to speak his mind without fear of the consequences. He provides his own physical security, economic security, food security, intellectual security and pretty much everything else. He has built the closest thing to a nation within a nation that we've seen in this country.

The descendants of our historical oppressors don't have the ability to tell Farrakhan what he can and cannot say. Countless celebrities and black public figures consult with the minister in private, primarily because they are often prohibited from speaking with him in public. I've consulted with him myself on multiple occasions and find him to be extraordinary in public and in-person.

The reason Farrakhan can say what he wants is because he makes his own money and maintains his freedom that way. He's not a big shot because he got a job at some fancy corporation. He's not respected because someone gave him a TV show. He's not beloved because he was elected to public office.

People love Farrakhan because he has FREEDOM and true POWER. It's not borrowed power or the illusion of freedom that comes with being propped up by someone else. It's the real power you obtain by building organizations from the ground up and nurturing them for the next generation.

Farrakhan has been able to do more for African-American men than anybody in the country, or any system in America. He works with men like Father Michael Pfleger, head pastor at St. Sabina church in Chicago, to go places where most politicians will not go, helping people that have long been forgotten by the rest of the city.

The second New Paradigm forum we held was in Washington, D.C. with Dr. Steve Perry. Dr. Perry happens to be somewhat conservative, which is fine with me. Some people take issue with black conservatives, and I'm not sure why. The truth is that our alignment with various political parties has done nothing to advance the cause of black people over the last 50 years. We are often used as political pawns in a game between the wealthy elite, much to our demise. Dr. Perry also happens to be an extraordinary educator, serving as the principal of The Capital Preparatory Magnet School in Hartford, Connecticut. He too agrees with the idea of black people being free to control our own destiny.

Our future is not one that is going to be given to us by the Democratic Party. In fact, they can go to hell. Our future is not going to be given to us by the Republican Party, they can go to hell too.

Our future is going to be created and built by us. It's not going to be granted to us by any politician, no matter how friendly they are to the African-American community. One of the reasons that Dr. Perry and I are aligned in our thinking is that, despite any political affiliations, we both have a deep, sincere and unapologetic love for our people.

DEMISE- MEANSA
PERSON'S DEATH.

14

It Takes a Village to Raise the Bar

Our third new paradigm forum was in New York City with respected scholar and activist, Dr. Cornel West. The reason I chose Dr. West for the forum is because Dr. West, whether you like him or not, is committed to poor people, black people and brown people like no one else.

If you'll notice, there are very few celebrities in America who are speaking up on behalf of black, brown, poor and incarcerated Americans. Instead, we have the black aristocracy that focuses on making their money and getting mainstream attention while doing almost nothing for the black community. In fact, many of our most cherished black public figures won't even let the word "black" come out of their mouths. That's disgusting and embarrassing, and We shouldn't allow ,nor accept that.

But so many of us are accustomed to seeing ourselves as second class citizens that we quietly sit in the back of the room and allow mainstream celebrities to give nothing back to their people.

Recently, the rapper Dr. Dre gave $35 million dollars to The University of Southern California (USC). This donation means very little to USC, since their endowment already exceeds the funding of every HBCU in America COMBINED. USC doesn't hire black professors very often. They rarely accept any black student who can't throw a football or dribble a basketball.

Dr. Walter Kimbrough, the president at Dillard University, wrote an open letter asking Dr. Dre why he wouldn't consider giving at least a fraction of that massive gift to an HBCU. Black colleges produce far more doctors, lawyers and professors than USC, with a much smaller budget. While USC barely sneezes at a $35 million dollar donation, such a gift to black students would have instantly transformed thousands of lives for the better.

Also, Dr. Dre has spent the last 25 years profiting from the death and chaos that has consumed the black community since the War on Drugs started in the 1970s, so it only seems logical that he be expected to

15 What Does aristocracy mean? The highest class in A society

give something back to the community that he has been allowed to mercilessly exploit for hundreds of millions of dollars in profit.

On our blogs, there were hundreds of thousands of African-Americans who not only understood why Dr. Kimbrough wrote his open letter, but supported and applauded it. However, there were just as many who felt that celebrities like Dr. Dre owe nothing to the black community. They were even offended by Dr. Kimbrough's suggestion, as if donating to the education of black children was somehow a meaningless endeavor.

This is the kind of slave-like thinking that has to be squashed in our community. Other ethnic groups did not prosper by promoting their own genocide and deflecting the value of education. A group of people cannot prosper by dumping the collective in favor of the greedy, selfish individual. We can't applaud black celebrities who extract billions in wealth from the black community and transfer the bulk of that wealth right back into the hands of the very same Europeans who are putting our young men and women in prison.

This is a form of mental illness, like an animal that eats its young, or a man who cuts out his own heart. This kind of thinking is the product of the effective and repetitive brainwashing that has consumed the black community since we arrived on slave ships many years ago. We would rather allow a corporation to pay us to die than to fight our oppressors in order to have a chance to live.

While many believe celebrities owe us nothing, we give them everything. I do not agree with this philosophy. I'm not impressed by how much money a celebrity makes or how much fame they have. I don't care how much validation you've received from the white community that may have convinced you that you're better than other black people.

We have to judge our celebrities by the content of their character, and not the size of their bank accounts. This transformation in thinking is critically important.

WEALTH

Now let's talk about the first component of the new paradigm: Wealth. When it comes to wealth, I humbly submit that I know what I'm talking about. I have a PhD in Finance. I spent 20 years teaching Finance at the college level, and 25 years studying the field.

One of the things that I can tell you beyond any doubt is that the vast majority of oppression and disenfranchisement in America is driven by economic inequality. Economic inequality exists because there were 400 years in which white Americans were allowed to steal our wealth and keep us from accumulating resources, thus leaving us almost nothing to pass down to our children. Today, not only do we have very little wealth, we are also addicted to excessive consumerism.

Your money is your power, yet African-Americans have been trained to give all of our power away. Destructive and gluttonous consumerism is planted into our brains by major corporations nearly every single day of our lives. They seek to control your mind in a multitude of ways, and they analyze you the same way a lion studies its prey. Those of us who are the least educated about these marketing/mind control techniques are typically the most vulnerable. We then end up giving our money to corporations that give us almost nothing back and won't even hire black people when they have open positions.

This has to stop.

When it comes to wealth, I've created something called the COST model. It means that in order to be free, you must be willing to pay the cost of your own freedom. This is an acronym that you can keep in mind on your own quest toward psychological, spiritual and economic freedom.

The "C" in the word "Cost" stands for Contribute. Everyone must contribute to some black institution other than your church. This means that every month, find something that you believe in and give money to it. I don't care how much it is, just get into the habit of giving something.

The point here is that we must all realize that in order for us to receive, we must remind ourselves to give. It's not that hard; people have already been conditioned to give to their churches, and only a small, logical step is necessary to begin giving to your community.

If we do not support our institutions, then nobody else will. We are a community that is addicted to the idea of expecting other people to maintain our institutions. Can you imagine if Jewish Synagogues were owned and financed by Nazis? What if the National Organization for Women was financially supported by Playboy Magazine? This is how silly we look when we assume that black institutions can be financially supported by other ethnic groups and not have to bow down to these entities at the drop of a hat.

If you wonder why the National Association for the Advancement of Colored People (NAACP) no longer fights for your rights as much as you would like, it's because the NAACP is not funded by black people. If black people aren't paying their bills, then why should they represent African-Americans over other constituencies? Do you really think that a corporation is going to give money to the NAACP so that the NAACP can attack that very same organization when they are caught being racist? Hell no!

Many corporations pay civil rights organizations as protection from scrutiny for their racist behavior. They believe, accurately, that if they give enough money to black leaders, they can abuse black people without suffering the consequences.

We've got to grow out of this line of thinking. If someone else is paying your bills, then they are going to make the rules. That's a simple fact of life that your grandmother probably told you when you were 10 years old.

The "O" in the COST model stands for ownership. Every black person in America must OWN something.

You start by owning your own home. Maybe you can own your own business. You've got to own something.

I don't care how much money you make; Freedom has a value of it's own, and you can't always compare yourself to someone who has had everything handed to him by his oppressor. The man or woman who owns something has assets they can transfer to their children, which can be built upon for future generations. Many of the great fortunes of America were built over several generations, not by people who kept starting over by following sloppy consumption and reproductive patterns.

If you own nothing, then you typically have nothing. Understanding the importance of ownership is one of the keys to black liberation, both economic and otherwise.

Everyone must own something in order to get ahead in America.

So, if you earn a lot of money and live paycheck-to-paycheck, spending like crazy on the latest and most fashionable consumer items, you're going to look back on your financial trail of tears only to realize that you've got nothing to show for it. Don't think like a consumer, think like an investor. That is how you get ahead financially.

"S"stands for save and invest.

You do not want to be a perpetual borrower and a spender in this economy because that is what corporations train you to do. I speculate that one of the reasons why financial literacy is not taught in high school is because they don't want Americans to be financially literate.

Right after the start of the economic crisis in 2008, government officials wanted to stimulate the economy. To do this, they gave every consumer 600 extra dollars for spending money, in hopes that they would put the money back into the economy by buying things with it.

Financial expert Suze Orman irritated government officials by going onto the Oprah Winfrey Show and telling the audience not to spend the money, but to save it instead. This was good advice for consumer survival, but not what corporations and our government officials wanted to hear.

Black people rarely receive the jobs that are created in this economy, but the fact is that we are among the greatest job creators. Millions of the jobs created in the American economy are built on the backs of black consumers because we are so good at giving our money away.

Even worse, many of these jobs are not being created in America. They're actually being created overseas. Overseas workers are the ones making the money and corporations are the ones extracting the profits. That's why the economic recovery has been so lopsided, with the middle and lower classes being left behind while corporations and stock holders are getting wealthier every day.

Corporations have gotten wealthier than ever over the last several years, and the working and middle classes have actually suffered because most of their wealth is tied up in the values of their homes. Many consumers don't even have a home, making their situation that much worse. Too many of us are excessive consumers, whereas for

irritated means= Borthering A Nerve in some one or Being Annoying corporations and the wealthy, a large percentage of their money is in the stock market. The growth in the stock market has a direct link to the growth in their wealth.

You should be a part of this money train, too. One way to join the train is to put yourself in the class of owners in this economy. Investing in the stock market is a good way to benefit from the market's dramatic rise. Don't just consider yourself to be a victim of corporate profiteering; position yourself to get some of that money, too.

You must save and invest your money so that you can own something, and then you will have the ability to contribute to your community. When you own the land on which you stand, you will find that your freedom will be multiplied 10 fold because no one can tell you what to do. You no longer have a reason to be afraid of whites, because whites will no longer be in charge of your access to happiness, legitimacy, prosperity and fulfillment.

The best way for me to control another man is for that man to know that I'm the reason that he gets to eat every day. If I know that, then that man will never disobey me. This is what happens to black Americans when we depend on racist institutions to feed our children. This is yet another form of mental illness that has been planted into us since slavery, because only a complete idiot depends on his oppressor to give him what he needs to survive.

"T" stands for Target. We must target our money carefully and not give it to just anybody who asks for it.

When you obtain wealth in the black community, you must target that wealth toward black businesses, black institutions, and other things that are going to help your community. I find it fascinating that there are people who will complain about spending $10 with a black company because they don't trust the business and don't know where the money is going. However, that same person will go to Walmart and spend $200 without asking a single question.

Walmart makes it very clear that they're not going to do anything for your community, yet many of us give them our money willingly. However, when a black business asks for a $10 purchase, we act like they're insane. You don't want to give the black-owned company a few bucks, but you're going to give hundreds to businesses that are run by racist people who don't even hire black employees.

That's a sick mentality. It's pathetic. It's an embarrassment to all of us.

Even if that business isn't going to use all of your money toward the stated objective, you can afford to make the investment anyway. Think about how often and how easily you might spend $10 on something else: popcorn and a drink at the movies, a quarter-tank of gas, or a couple of drinks at a restaurant. Why wouldn't you give that same amount to something that will benefit the people you claim to love?

My argument is that every black child in America must learn the value of entrepreneurship, even if they never run a business of their own. It's like knowing how to hunt, fish and build just in case there is a disaster. Then, as the rest of us learn the value of targeting our resources, we then have the ability to create black jobs, sustain black jobs and eventually OBTAIN black jobs. Targeting always goes full circle.

The black community is consistently bombarded by economic disasters, and often finds itself at the receiving end of untold amounts of financial torture. Black men are virtually eliminated from the economic system, and relegated to the undignified position of begging for jobs and hoping that some white man will give him a tiny opportunity. Most white kids prosper, live happy lives, raise families and go to summer camp. Too many of our children struggle, endure trauma, and have kids out of wedlock that we can't afford to feed.

This has to stop. We've got to learn how to create our own jobs and make our own money. I'm tired of begging other people to get what we need. I'm sick of black men having to do a minstrel dance and keep their heads low in order to get corporate opportunities. I'm tired of us waiting for another group of people to validate us and give us their stamp of approval before we are allowed to believe that we are worthy.

I'm sick of it.

Entrepreneurship is typically not something that you're taught in school, it is something that good parents build into the souls of their children) In a way, you can compare it to being able to grow your own economic food, instead of depending on someone else to feed you. It gives you freedom in the event of disaster, or in the case that you decide that you simply want something better out of life than enduring the stress of doing work that you actually hate.

Think for a second about just how vulnerable you are when you depend on someone else to give you the things you need. In fact, imagine if your family needed food, and the only person supplying the food was your worst enemy. The food wouldn't come for free, nor would it be easy to obtain. Your enemy would feed his children long before he chose to feed yours. The cost for obtaining the food would be high, and you would only be fed if you did what your financial master told you to do.

In the scenario I just described, you would either be stressed out or hungry. You would be without dignity. You would be disrespected because no one respects a man who has to beg in order to feed his family.   You wouldn't be truly living your life, you would only be surviving and waiting to die. Even if you were to receive everything you needed, there is a very good chance you would be MISERABLE.

That's where black people are in America when we depend on White America to feed us. We get jobs with big corporations and then get angry because they subject us to discrimination.   We wonder why our unemployment rate is twice as high as whites, yet virtually no government official has tried to help alleviate the problem.   We express outrage that economic inequality has not dissipated since the 1960s, yet we continue to pursue the same weak, tired and ineffective economic models.

When you gain the ability to create jobs, you don't have to beg for them. When you run your own enterprise, you don't have to worry about racism. Instead, you have the ability to do what you want, when you want, and not feel that you're trying to become comfortable under somebody else's roof.

When I learned to run my own business, that's when racism effectively disappeared from my life. Of course, it still exists in some situations, like when dealing with police, trying to obtain financing or obtaining white customers. But when it comes to my day-to-day existence, I am constantly marveling over how stress-free my life has become. I get to take freedoms for granted everyday that some of my corporate friends can only dream of. I can say what I want, do what I want, work when I want, and make my own money.

In fact, my new life after working for somebody else was such an improvement that I usually don't care if I make a little less money than I expected. I was just happy to get off the economic plantation and go to work each day feeling like a MAN. You really can't put a price on freedom.

Most entrepreneurs in America choose their profession because they had a parent who told them that they should start their own business. Those little words being uttered by a parent can shape the entire trajectory of a child's future.

Tell your children they should have their own businesses, even if you don't have a business yourself. Teach them the value of OWNERSHIP, even if you don't own as much as you'd like. Have them read this book and memorize it to give them strength in adulthood. Those little seeds you plant in your child's brain will form roots and structures that are greater than anything you could ever imagine.

(Even more importantly, make sure that you and your children are never tempted to measure success in purely financial terms.) White people have all the money, so by evaluating ourselves based on a resource that they possess in abundance, we are effectively giving them all the power and promoting white supremacy in the process. It's like judging yourself by how blue your eyes are or how blonde your hair is. Never become dependent on a resource that you do not control.

Finally, you never want your children to believe that the only way to become somebody in this world is to bend and fold to the whims of people who may never respect you. Teach them to have values and integrity. Help them decide where they would like to take a stand. If you don't help them to build their ethical center, they will constantly morph themselves into little robots who simply follow the value system of those who have the most money.

Teach your children the COST model when they are very young, and then put them into programs that will allow them to learn how to make their own money.

Teaching your children how to make money isn't enough. They can hoard all the money in the world, but it means almost nothing if you've raised them to be selfish. Instead, raise your children to know that wealth-building is important for their individual success as well as the success of those they care about. After they've accumulated some economic opportunities, it is then important to multiply those opportunities by investing in black businesses, hiring black employees and giving to black organizations. By sharing, teaching, building and lifting, you are able to take individual wealth and convert that into collective wealth. In return, these new opportunities will help your child to gain wealthy black allies, since people tend to support those who've supported them in the past.

Remember what I said earlier: You must know how to make your own money in the same way you might learn how to grow your own food. Black unemployment is chronically high, and this is not going to change anytime in the near future. It's not logical to expect that black and white Americans are *ever*going to achieve parity in the unemployment rate, at least not while whites own nearly all of the businesses. Those who don't know how to cook typically get to eat last. The only solution is to either create a black-owned business, or at least make sure you're supporting as many of these businesses as you possibly can. Something has GOT to change.

Let's talk about our sons. Black males have the highest unemployment rate in America. If black men cannot provide for their families, they typically do not want to get married. The economic pressure is overwhelming for many of these brothers in large part because so many of them have been marginalized by the criminal justice system. For some men, if they can't provide for themselves, they may even end up *wanting*to go back to prison. At the very least, some may not feel that they belong anyplace else

A black man in prison has an almost impossible time being an active and involved husband and father. It is difficult to run a household when you are either incarcerated or trying to stay one step ahead of the cops. It's also difficult to take care of other people if you can't find a job, can't pay your bills, and have no education or opportunity. So, economic stability is deeply connected to family stability. In order for the black community to rise, we must help the black man to get back on his feet and stay there.

The economy has shifted for all Americans. The days of working for one corporation for 20 years and getting a guaranteed retirement plan are gone. Now, companies will fire you in a second. For your own economic security, even if you work for somebody else, you should have your own business on the side. If you don't have your own business, then join some sort of economic cooperative which will allow you to invest in someone else's business.

A cooperative investing situation might mean joining with other like-minded people, pooling your resources and investing in a venture at the same time. Even if you're all getting a paycheck, there is no reason that a consistent fraction of that paycheck can't go toward building your path off the economic plantation.

Even if you don't want to be a full-time entrepreneur, you still have the opportunity to own something that belongs to you. Find a black business and invest in it. Being an owner, even a minority silent partner, gives you a secondary source of income outside your job. This is another place where wealth is being created in America, and you want to be a part of it.

EDUCATION

The next tenant of the new paradigm is education. Let me say this very clearly: When you walk away from economic responsibility and walk away from educational opportunity, you are walking right into the hands of *slavery*.

There is a reason that our ancestors were told many years ago that they would not be allowed to read without the penalty of incarceration or even death.

The reason that America has always feared an educated black populous is because education is POWER. Literacy is power. Critical thinking skills are a form of power. African-Americans are not meant to have power in this country. That is part of the reason that the system works so hard to ensure that African-American children are not given an adequate opportunity to be properly educated.

In many inner cities across America, black children are forced to attend inferior schools that don't have the same materials as schools that educate whites. When you visit suburban schools, you find the latest computers, textbooks and Olympic-size swimming pools. When you visit black neighborhoods, you will often find teachers who are overworked and underpaid, and unable to give the students the things they need.

What's even worse than not educating African-Ar society gives them the illusion of education. I educated, many of us are indoctrinated. Miseduca worse than no education at all, and it's become a form of psychological Ebola. When you go to school year after year and are taught a bunch of lies, you're being trained to see the world in a way that makes you a highly effective slave to those who've been given the opportunity to brainwash you.

I know a lot of people with MDs, PhDs, MBAs and JDs who can't exactly explain why their education makes the world a better place. Many of them do what they do every day primarily because of money.

Many of us who are educated at predominantly white public schools and universities are taught to believe that the key to salvation is to go to school for a very long time so you can one day work for a benevolent white person. The angry black middle class mostly consists of black people who played the game the right way, made what they thought were all the right decisions, and found themselves feeling as powerless as a person can feel without actually being dead.

False educational indoctrination will train you to believe that every great thing ever done was built, designed and executed by a white man. You hear about the greatness of Europe and learn nothing about Africa. You are told that the foundations of mathematics and science started in ancient Greece and hear nothing about the amazing things done by people of color throughout the world.

You may be led to believe that the greatest thing a black person has ever done is to be freed by a white person. Black history in public school typically consists of slavery, the Emancipation Proclamation, Martin Luther King and President Barack Obama. Everything else is just a blur.

Not only does the school system lie to you, you're taught to be handicapped: Deep down, your child is thoroughly convinced that almost nothing good in all of black history could ever have been accomplished without the support and consent of whites.

The person or institution that educates you effectively builds a cage for your mind. They decide how the cage is going to be shaped, how big it's going to be, the shape of the cage, what it looks like and of what material the cage is going to be made. Therefore, when you allow an institution controlled by your oppressor to educate your children, you are handing over their most valuable asset to the very people who are seeking to oppress them. What is their most valuable asset? Their mind.

When your kids turn on the radio and hear 10,000 messages stating that they are meant to be gangsters, thugs, killers and exceedingly promiscuous, they are indoctrinating your child into believing that they should aim to be something other than what God intended them to be. Rather than becoming an engineer, doctor, lawyer or business owner, the child then spends his life dodging jail time, dealing with depression, wasting money by "balling out", escaping through drug use and living in the unemployment line.

We must take responsibility for the education of our children. You cannot trust a system that is destroying black children by the boatload and expect it to give your child an adequate educational background. Millions of black parents are educating their children at home, even if their kids are still in public school during the day. Millions of black parents are turning off the radio and not allowing their kids to watch white-owned, racist television networks like BET and VH1.

Let me say this bluntly: The school system does *not* care about your child. The school-to-prison pipeline is 100% real, and prisons are being filled with African-Americans, primarily black males, because these young men are an extremely profitable commodity for the prison-industrial complex (Educated black men don't typically end up in prison,) because uneducated black men are the real targets of this heinous, corrupt system.

If you allow your child to be uneducated or even miseducated, there is a very good chance they will end up incarcerated.

Here's what we need to do right now.

Every black child in America MUST be homeschooled.

This means that even if your child goes to school someplace else, you have to use the evenings to educate your child properly. You must use the weekends to give your child the additional education that they need. You must use the summer to allow your child to be educated on the things that matter. This will allow that child to grow into a prosperous, happy, healthy adult.

You do not have to be an educated person in order to do any of this. The Internet provides many opportunities for education. You can have your child watch YouTube videos about science, mathematics and African-American history.

There are thousands of YouTube channels dedicated to teaching fundamental educational concepts at all levels. Most of these channels aren't run by black people, but that's OK. Having your child watch a few videos on chemistry or a cartoon about the basics of math can open the floodgates of knowledge to inspire your child to continue engaging in the important task of independent learning.

You can have your kids do reports for you on the Internet based on politics and business. Pay them to do the work if you have to, it's better than giving them an allowance for sweeping the floor. You can teach them yourself and help them learn the things they need to know to be productive and responsible adults. In fact, I suggest using this as an opportunity to learn together. Learning should be a lifelong process, not something that stops when you quit going to school.

A mind is a terrible thing to waste, and it's also a terrible thing to hand over to the descendants of your historical oppressors. DO NOT trust the school system to educate your kids.

When educating your own children, you can teach them the things you want them to know. You can teach your children how to invest. You can teach them how to own their own business. You can teach your child how to be a good husband, wife, father or mother. You can teach them all the things they need to know in order to survive in this society. They are typically not going to learn these things at school, so it is your job to teach them.

Education isn't just a bunch of information designed to fill your brain. It also shapes your culture, preferences, choices and the way you treat people. If a girl is educated on the principles of child-rearing, she's going to be a better mother. If a boy is educated on conflict resolution, he is going to be a better husband. If a child understands the dangers of drugs and alcohol, they are less likely to abuse drugs later on down the road.

Education is the key to shaping a life.

Let's re-emphasize the critical role of the parent. Some people want to blame all of the failings of the school system on inadequate teachers or inappropriate systems. But that's a liberal solution to a very complex problem. Don't let liberals or conservatives guide you away from common sense.

Common sense tells us that almost no child can be properly educated if his/her parents don't give a damn. In fact, a bad parent can ruin and undermine every good thing that a well-intended teacher might do in the life of a child. In fact, the most important teacher in the life of a child is the parent.

If the parent fails to do their job, then the child will be uneducated or miseducated, even if they go to school every day, and even if they make straight As. Understand and respect your role as a parent, for this is the key to your ability to shape, create and define universes. You could tell your child that the sky is green, and they would believe you. If you tell your daughter she's a queen, she's going to believe it. If you tell your son he's a thug, he's going to believe that, too.

Sometimes, the most powerful part of a child's mental development is their emotional and spiritual upbringing. I'm not talking about church, although that can be a part of it, if you prefer. Instead, I'm referring to the value systems, perspectives, and self-identity you instill in a child at an early age. Sometimes, more education can occur in one sentence than a thousand textbooks put together.

What I've found in my years of teaching and public work is that there are a whole bunch of black people with a boatload of education and no sense of community. They might know how to accumulate money, but don't know what to do with it. They might know how to obtain power, but don't use it for anything other than self-preservation. They know how to survive, but aren't willing to put their survival at risk for anything other than themselves. Many of us are among the walking dead: simply going from action-to-action, with no meaningful purpose other than getting enough money to pay this month's rent or to purchase some meaningless material possession that makes us feel like we're more accomplished, when in reality, we're more deeply embedding ourselves as slaves to a capitalist society.

So, education goes deeper than what you learn in a book. It actually consists of a set of deliberate strategies one might utilize in order to ensure that he or she is given the opportunity to live a truly meaningful life.

I was recently in a documentary called *Elementary Genocide*. Dr. Umar Johnson was another participant in the film, along with the rapper Killer Mike and many other interesting thought-leaders with important things to say. One of the points that Dr. Johnson made in the documentary is that if your son cannot read by the age of 10, there is a 75% chance that he will end up in prison by the age of 25.

The specifics of this statistic can vary, depending on the source, but the point remains the same: *Education can literally save your life.* Education can be the difference between a life of freedom and a life

34

of servitude. It not only has the functional task of giving you skills to have a chance to join the country's economic system, but it also can provide you with the critical-thinking and information-gathering capability necessary to keep you from being hoodwinked.

The school-to-prison pipeline is a very real holocaust. This is a very serious problem. This is a problem that will be solved with education. Honest, meaningful and culturally-relevant education must become the most important value in the African-American community, and it must become something that we are determined to give to our children.

The same way a good mother won't let her child spend the entire day covered in filth, no good parent should allow their child to live in ignorance.

We also need black people educating black children. The current educational system, unfortunately, is a lot like a plantation. White teachers are ruining the lives of black children every single day because many of them are unable to see their potential. Some of them see our children as criminals from the day they walk into the classroom, and this is especially true for black boys.

The fact is that the system fears your son. Another truth is that he is perceived to be a threat, especially if he is intelligent, fearless and proud. The goal of the educational system, as with most American institutions, is to break your son down and rebuild him in the image that appears to be most fit for that institution. This is one of the reasons that athletes are so poorly educated in American high schools and universities.

Since college and professional athletes are such a huge cash cow for corporate America, there is a special effort to keep them dumbed down and well-trained to assimilate. They are distracted with women, liquor, worthless trinkets, a little cash and a few other items, led to believe that their sole purpose in life is to maintain the great American minstrel show.

Many athletes are taught to believe that money and fame are worth the price of community empowerment, self-love, and intellectual freedom. Some athletes show up on college campuses unable to read and not wanting to learn. The institution itself serves as an accomplice in this extraordinary intellectual crime, which teaches that 18-year-old student-athlete that his job is to be a football player and nothing else.

Once again, in the case of the black athlete, the primary guardian is the parent. Since many of these young men do not have fathers in the home to guide them, the job is left to the mother and the primary male role model. If the job of guiding the young black male athlete is left to the coach, he's going to guide him to the football field or basketball court, not the classroom or the civil rights march. Athletes have so much power and prominence that universities and corporations won't dare allow their prized animals to become "hindered" with self-respect, educational achievement, community compassion or any of the other attributes that might get in the way of winning a championship.

But athletes aren't the only young black people being controlled by educational systems.

Like a plantation, many school systems actively work to keep children away from black people who are going to liberate and elevate their minds. The speakers who are invited to speak to your child are going to be those who promote a way of thinking that the institution deems to be "appropriate" for young black children. Because there are people who see blacks as inferior, they may feel that the best thing they can do for a young black man is to teach him to behave like a young white man.

If your child's disposition is not conducive to conformity and assimilation, there is a good chance that he will be subject to ostracism and punishment. I've seen countless young black kids, especially boys, punished just for being themselves. They are often forced to apologize for virtually nothing.   I understand this issue very well, since I was once one of those boys.

This constant berating destroys the child's self-esteem to the point where he is either going to decide to become a natural rebel or he's going to feel that there's something wrong with him.   Either way, your child will end up lost and looking for something to make them complete. When you're spending all of your time finding yourself, you don't get to spend very much time achieving, conquering, empowering and fighting for something meaningful. Instead, you're just stumbling along, trying to survive and hoping that life doesn't keep kicking you in the butt.

Do not allow your child to be taken away from you by the plantation. You must control the destiny of your offspring.

Here is another important fact. In the quest to educate our children, we must confront toxic hip-hop culture. We must confront the bastardization of hip-hop that has occurred, which is leading to messages that brainwash our kids into leaving their destinies behind.

If you're not listening to the music being mass-produced on the radio, you really need to take the time to inform yourself on what is going on.   Many of the messages in hip-hop music have been wired to provide blueprints for self-destruction.   In fact, I dare say that there is not a single person who can follow the lifestyle being marketed by most mainstream hip-hop artists and end up as anything other than a counter-productive alcoholic, "baby daddy," prison inmate or drug addict.

I don't fault most of the artists entirely for what's been happening, since many of them are young and don't understand the power of their words.   However, I hold record labels almost entirely accountable for providing financial support for messages that are deadly to young black people.

The music has different impacts on different kids, depending on their socioeconomic background. A child in the suburbs who hears a song about killing another black man isn't usually going to act on it. He's going to see the music as entertainment entirely, and a way to escape to a thugged-out fantasy that breaks away from the mundane life of a middle class American. At worst, he'll think that black people enjoy calling ourselves 'niggers' and 'bitches,' and that we love to act like monkeys on stage.

But in neighborhoods where guns can be bought cheaply without a parent's permission, toxic hip-hop often becomes the theme music for homicide. I once interviewed the rapper Dee-1, a conscious, talented and intelligent artist with a very powerful message. One thing he said during the interview was that when his best friend was murdered in a drive-by shooting, he knew that the men coming to kill him were probably not listening to love songs or country music. Any good psychologist will confirm that the music you put into your subconscious mind impacts the way you see yourself and the way you see the world. That's just a fundamental fact.

Hip-hop was once a powerful art form designed to empower people of color. It lifted our souls and made us into better people. It encouraged us to become politically-engaged. It pushed us to study black history. It made us aware of racism and despair occurring in our communities. Then it got turned into a poisonous minstrel show, like Ebola for the soul.

When hip-hop took a turn for the worse, it went from being a tool for empowering people to becoming a weapon being used to oppress us. If you listen to most hip-hop songs on the radio, within the first sixty seconds, you are likely to hear a message that promotes excessive drug and alcohol consumption, violence, misogyny, financial irresponsibility or sexual promiscuity.

Not one of these behaviors, if applied on a consistent basis, will lead to a healthy and prosperous life. In most cases, it will set you so far behind the rest of the world that you can't get ahead because you're spending all of your time catching up. It's the perfect recipe for the spiritual and psychological extermination of young black people, and the truth is that *it's working*.

When you look in the black community, you see that young black people are leading the country in STD infections; we're leading the nation in homicides, most of them being black-on-black. We're leading the nation in the proportion of uneducated and miseducated people. We are getting worse with each generation when it comes to drug and alcohol abuse, since every young black boy is pressured into believing that he's supposed to smoke and drink from the time he gets out of bed in the morning.

The problem with the consumption of drugs and alcohol is that it destroys our future leaders, especially young black men. A man who smokes weed all day doesn't usually have the energy to go out and conquer the world, he's more likely to sit at home and feel sorry for himself. If you're too busy chasing instant gratification or the next high, you won't be getting high from the excitement of making your world into a better place. If you're drowning in ignorance, you will never know the power of flying with intelligence.

We have to stop this trend in its tracks, or at the very least, stop behaving like this is normal. We cannot allow the worst of the rap music industry to continue to destroy our children. This means that within your household, you have to talk to your children about these influences to make sure that they do not stick to their psyches. You may have to turn off the radio. You may also have to join national movements that are fighting to confront major radio conglomerates and record labels for their decision to profit off of the promotion of genocidal messages.

As a community, we have to confront and shut down those individuals and corporations who see our collective death as one of their many profit centers. Understand there is no other genre of music in existence anywhere in which women are more disrespected than they are in hip-hop. There's no genre of music anywhere that promotes the idea of black men killing other people who look like them. There's no genre of music anywhere that promotes drug and alcohol consumption the way toxic hip-hop does. There's no genre of music anywhere that glorifies a lack of education or incarceration.

This package of self-destruction was designed specifically for YOU and it's catered to put your children in a prison cell or a casket.

Toxic hip-hop has become unique in many regards, reaching a level of destructiveness that boggles the mind. Unfortunately, it is an example of big racist corporations that are making a profit because they've convinced us to sing and dance to the beat of our own genocide.

FAMILY

The third tenet of the new paradigm for black America has to do with family. The family unit is one of the most important components of any community. If you want to destroy a community, you can start by destroying the family. If you want to destroy the family, you can start by destroying the man. The black man, for the last forty years, has been killed by this society: Many of our men have become addicted to drugs, killed over drugs, incarcerated over drugs and left unemployed and uneducated. Of course there are exceptions to this rule, but for many communities, this has become the norm.

I cannot tell you how many times I've gone to black events in "the hood" and quietly wondered where the young men have gone.   A young lady that I mentor even asked me if I knew anyone who was married. She was absolutely serious! In a grim tone of voice, she said, "Do you know anybody who's married? I don't know anybody who's married?"

Apparently, all of the girl's friends at school lived with their mothers and half of them had no idea who their fathers were. This is NOT normal.

Another young lady I mentor said that not one of her friends has a father in the home. She went on to become a young single mother to a man who had three kids with two other women by the age of 22. So, the creation of self-destructive cycles in our families is leaving us broke, traumatized and devastated. We must be honest about this.

I wish I had a nickel for every young mother I've met who'd relegated herself to the status of "baby mama" before the child was even born. Part of this comes from the fact that so many black men have been trained to be "playas" and "pimps" before deciding that they might want to become husbands or fathers. Too many black women have been trained to judge a man by the car he drives, the "swag" he possesses or the way he thrusts his sex organs. Apparently, evaluating potential mates by the content of their character has become old-fashioned.

Fathers in many black families have simply gone out of style. Many mothers don't believe they need them, and too many men are convinced that their presence isn't necessary. Even worse, we now have white liberals seeking to convince us that this is OK.

I'm sorry, but it's not. Fathers are protectors of their children and the household. Thousands of children are molested every year by their mother's boyfriends because their fathers aren't in the home to protect them.

Strong men are built to be natural providers. One of the greatest indicators of poverty is whether or not two parents are in the household. When you have two earners, you have more money to take care of the family. You have someone to depend on when things go wrong. You have another person around to watch the kids to make sure they are safe. You can try to do everything by yourself, but you're probably going to do it WRONG.

A lot of young girls are taking on male identities because some of them feel that they must become men in order to protect themselves from the men who've hurt them in the past. The job of protecting the black woman should lie with the black man. We can't rely on society to do it for us, because the evidence says they won't.

Boys aren't being raised to become men because so many of them are being coddled by their mothers. These man-boys are too weak to take a leadership role in a household themselves because they've never been taught to do so. Manhood must be taught by another man, the same way only a woman can teach true womanhood. When a woman tries to build a man, she usually does it in the wrong way. Her intentions are always good, but the outcomes are usually suboptimal. It's not until the boy fails to be an adequate head of another woman's household that the mother looks back and realizes that he never learned to be the kind of man that another woman might need to protect her own children.

The same would be true if I'd tried to teach my daughter how to do her hair, pick out the right outfits or put on a tampon. No matter how hard I try to convince myself that I know how to be a woman, the fact is that I would end up screwing her up for life. She would never learn the subtleties of being a woman. She might never know how to deal with the opposite sex in a healthy way. She would probably have a tough time being a wife to another man, because she might be accustomed to allowing me to have too much control over her life (I'm sure you've seen mothers who treat their sons like they are imaginary husbands).

I don't know about you, but I find it offensive that we sit quietly and smile politely while others impose an agenda on our community that is making it nearly impossible for young, intelligent black women to even find a husband. Black women deserve to have protectors and providers. But men must be trained to fill that role. Simultaneously, women must be trained to expect and respect that role when such a man becomes available to them. You cannot solve such a complex problem in a vacuum.

But here's the thing: It's not the black man's fault that so many of our men have become weak and so many of our women have come to hate some of us. When I did research on the impact of the War on Drugs, I could see, without a doubt, just how much these seemingly innocuous policy changes have destroyed our community.

Ever since the War on Drugs began in 1971, we've seen a tremendous spike in the incarceration rates of African-American men. We saw situations where black Americans were impacted by drugs on every level. We were the ones getting addicted. We were the ones being incarcerated. We were the ones being killed in violence related to narcotics. We were also the ones being traumatized by the things happening to those around us, much of which occurred because of drugs.

There are millions of black children who are now dysfunctional adults because one or both of their parents was hooked on drugs.

There are millions of children who grew up without fathers because their providers/protectors were serving time in American labor camps (prisons).

There are millions of young people who were introduced to drugs and/or violence at an early age, and it may have led to their own death or incarceration.

Millions of young people are affected by the mental illness which comes from being abused at an early age.

What has happened is that two generations of the black community have been absolutely *obliterated* by public policy that has been no less impactful than the Holocaust that murdered six million Jews during World War II. In order for us to clean up this mess and move forward as a community, we are going to have to redefine ourselves and start from the beginning to make sure that we promote values in our community that are consistent with the importance of the family.

The first value that we must reclaim is the importance of the father in the household. You have hyper-liberal, extreme feminists, who have convinced millions of black women that fathers don't matter. Many feminists, unfortunately, do not respect black men. They do not want to promote policies that will strengthen the black family. They are just fine with seeing black men dead, incarcerated or outside of the home.

Some of these nasty detractors are the same white females who punish your black son in the school system because they don't understand him. They are the ones who benefit from affirmative action in the workplace, but then wag their finger at you when you attempt to get black men hired on the job. They are the ones who tell black women that the answer to all of their problems is to stop pursuing black men and simply date outside your race.

People have convinced far too many African-Americans that the father does not matter. Many Americans perceive the cultural idiosyncrasies of black men to be crass, degrading, ignorant and barbaric. In fact, I've rarely seen any extreme white feminist speak out on issues that affect black men. For example, if feminists are fighting on behalf of rape victims, why not speak out against prison rape? If you're fighting against domestic abuse, why not speak out on behalf of men who are victims of domestic violence as well?

Black women deserve to be respected, exalted and treated with the utmost dignity at all times. Black men who see black women being disrespected have an obligation to speak up about it. The lack of trust between black men and women is partially built upon the fact that many black women no longer feel that they can trust us to respect and protect them. This is where men must never fall short.

At the same time, black women must always remember the importance of respecting men. Most women want to be loved, and most men want to be supported and empowered as kings of their households. When a man is being beaten down emotionally, emasculated at every turn and constantly told that there is something wrong with him, you're creating the very kind of man that you would never want to be in a relationship with.

In many of these strained black relationships, the mother was raised in a household where the father wasn't there. Rather than the father being an important and critical component of the life of that child, the mother might have seen the father as an inconvenient accessory that she may or may not choose to keep in her home. She might be convinced that she can remove the father from her household with no cost to herself, her child or the rest of her family.

We have to realize that fathers are just as important as mothers in the lives of our children. Anybody who tells us that the father is not a valuable part of a child's life does not care about the black family. In fact, they are an enemy to the black community.

Fathers must understand how important they are to the black family as well. Many young men don't believe they need to be in the lives of their children because they didn't have a father in their own life. They think that fathers are also optional accessories.

Let's be clear: Fatherhood should never be optional. If you are man enough to lie down and have sex with a woman, then you should be man enough to take care of that child until the age of 18.   The psychological damage imposed on a child by a missing father is both painful and unforgiveable. A father should do all he can to remain in the lives of his children.

If you are woman enough to decide that you want to sleep with a man, then you need to be woman enough to make sure that man has the opportunity to be as fully-invested in the life of his child as you are. You do not own your child. Nobody owns the child independently. It is a 50-50 partnership. We have to understand this if we want to keep our families together. Children typically suffer when they don't have a structured family environment. This is a fact.

The other thing that many of us must realize is that you don't have to have a child in order to be a parent. Right now, in our community, we need a parenthood bailout. We need individuals who care about the black community to step in and intervene in the lives of children when they see that those kids are suffering. We need fathers to step to the plate and protect young children who need their protection.

We need mothers to step to the plate to love and nurture those children who need love and support.

From this point on, we must reclaim the village and remember that we are all soldiers in this battle. Whether or not you believe that a battle is occurring right now doesn't matter, because war has already been declared on us. It was declared on us forty years ago and has been declared on us since we arrived in this country hundreds of years ago.

The other important thing to understand for your own life is that if you believe in the value of the black family, you must detach from the limited short-term thinking that exists in many African American relationships. A lot of people get married, but should probably never do it. They don't understand the first thing about love and what it means to stick it out and make a relationship work. They get married and say "Until death do us part," but really what they mean is "Until I get tired of being with this person, find myself uncomfortable and want to be with somebody else."

Well, guess what? If you don't understand how to stay married and how to keep a family together, then you shouldn't start a family if you're just going to break it up. If you want your family to last, go study how to make a family last. Read books on conflict resolution. Read books on how to choose a proper mate. Read books on how to raise a child. Take a class on child rearing so you can raise your child properly. Stop shooting from the hip. Study the things that you need to know in order to be a productive and responsible parent.

So many people engage in the important task of motherhood or fatherhood and don't even take the time to learn how to do it the right way. If you were taught the wrong approach, then you probably won't know how to do it the right way. If you grew up without a father in the household, you will probably have a hard time keeping a father in your household unless you learn what it takes to keep a man in your house. If a man has never seen what a father does everyday, he will probably have a tough time figuring it all out later on down the road. If we want our families to stick together, we have to learn how to make the adjustments necessary for us to co-exist with other human beings.

Making a family last is no different from committing yourself to any other goal in life, like finishing medical school or losing a lot of weight. It requires patience, discipline, focus, and even tenacity. It's also something you can learn how to do by reading articles on the Internet.

We have to be able to do what our grandparents did when they were able to stay married for 40 or 50 years. We can no longer allow for the ridiculous trend where a father is out of the life of a child by the time the child is 6 months old, or the marriage ends within 6 months of the day you signed the marriage certificate. These habits are weak. They are also immature. This is embarrassing. This is pathetic. We have to do better for ourselves as a community because if we don't get the black family together, then we will never get the black community together, and that is a fact.

Civil rights leaders can only do so much. The Democratic Party will do even less. No one is coming to save us, and we have to accept that. If you can't save yourself in this world, then you have nothing. That's a reality that we must face.

COMMUNITY

The last component of the New Paradigm is community. In order for us to become strong as a people, we must understand the importance of maintaining a sense of community. A sense of community means that you are committed to giving and living for something that is bigger than yourself. We can't survive if all of us are selfish. We can't survive if none of us feels the necessity to give back to the people we care about. We cannot survive if all of our most talented and brilliant doctors, lawyers, professors, athletes and entertainers are constantly giving to somebody else but giving nothing to their own people. We cannot survive if we don't learn the importance and the value of sticking together.

When we had the new paradigm forum with Minister Louis Farrakhan, one of the things that he brought up, which I agreed with, is that African-Americans can learn a great deal from the Jewish community. Because of what the Jewish community has endured, they are deeply committed to sticking together and supporting one another. They pool their resources. They educate their own children. They support each other politically. They are in the habit of working together, and because they keep a solid core, it is very difficult for anyone to exploit people in that community.

This can be the future for black America. It's not going to happen with everybody. Some people committed to the slave mentality are going to have to be left behind. Some of those individuals are going to have to be cast out of the brilliant future that our community will possess. I am an eternal optimist when it comes to the future of black America. I believe, without a doubt, that the future belongs to us.

But while I am optimistic, I am also a realist. I know that right now, those who care about the black community are not necessarily those who have the most power. As it stands, ignorance is winning. Ignorance is what's being promoted on the radio. Ignorance is what's being taught in schools. Ignorance is what has become popular among our children. There are millions of us who believe in a better future for our people. There are millions of us who are deeply determined to educate ourselves and empower our people so that the future for our grandchildren is better than the present that we're living today.

As a community, I suggest that we lean on the tradition of the runaway slave. We have to remember that there will probably never be a day when you will see the bulk of the benefits from your contribution. There will never be a day where you won't turn on the TV and hear about a black child who has been slaughtered. There will never be a day where you won't turn on the radio and hear some Negro spouting all kinds of ignorance that is designed to destroy black people. Better days may never arrive in your lifetime. But you're not doing this for yourself. You're making this sacrifice for your children, your grandchildren and your great-grandchildren so that they can live a better life than us.

The key for the development of our community is not just unity, but to remember that we have an obligation to protect our children from all enemies, both foreign and domestic. This means that we have an internal expectation to protect our children from racist oppressors, as well as anyone who seeks to harm them.

We also have an obligation to protect our children from people of color who have sold out to higher interests, or who have been indoctrinated into a way of thinking that is poisonous and destructive. These cultural zombies have to be dealt with and annihilated no differently from the way we had to deal with black overseers on the plantation. We can still love these people, and we don't have to physically harm them, but it is also okay to cast out those selfish individuals who don't feel that they owe anything to their community.

When you hear about a celebrity who says "I don't owe anything to black people. All I want to do is go out and buy gold chains and diamonds and fancy cars for myself," that celebrity should be castigated. We need to humiliate that person. We need to boycott that person. We need to let that person know that if you don't feel that you owe anything to the black community, then the black community will decide that it owes nothing to you. Everyone must contribute in order for a family to survive and prosper.

This leads me to the state of the prominent black male.

The physical and intellectual power of the black male can be compared to that of an elephant in a circus. The trainer knows that if the elephant ever realizes his power, he can crush him with just one foot. So, the goal of the trainer is to ensure that the elephant never realizes who is bigger, who is stronger and who is more powerful.

By giving the elephant electric shocks at an early age, intimidating him, providing selective rewards and punishments, the trainer effectively brainwashes the elephant into believing that he is less powerful than the tiny man who is telling him what to do. He never wants the elephant to see other elephants rise up, for this might educate the elephants on how quickly their situation would change if they were to all stick together. So, the goal is to not only keep the elephant intimidated and frightened, but to even fool the elephant into believing that the trainer is his best friend.

The greatest fear of the trainer is that one day, the elephant is going to wake up and realize just how strong he is. He may also gain a hunger for his own freedom and a realization that he doesn't need the trainer in order to survive. Even worse, the trainer fears that the elephant will never forget the torture, terrorism and manipulation that was used to keep the elephant under control, all so he could selfishly earn his profit.

On that fateful day, the tables will be turned forever.

Black people react angrily when we find out about the torture of our ancestors, which was never taught to us in school. We become a mighty force when we stand up, stick together and refuse to make meaningless compromises. When we engage in the mental strength training needed to overcome our oppressive condition, we become as powerful as elephants trampling trainers on their way out of the circus.

This is my dream for black America.

We need to move toward self-sufficiency. Get away from this idea of integration as the key to your salvation, because it's not. Let me be extremely clear when I say this to you: Complete cultural, educational and economic integration is **not** the solution for black people. Integration has harmed black people more than it has helped them.

Dr. King was an amazing man who achieved wonderful things in his lifetime. He did the right thing for the era in which he was living. He was able to run the first 100 meters of a 400-meter relay race, and it's up to us to carry the baton for the rest of the race.

Now it is time for us to take the game to another level. Sometimes, to move forward, you've got to go back. When I say go back, I mean we have to go back to the days where we understood that we must educate our own children.

We must learn to make our own money. We must support our own community. We must protect and defend the psyches and the spirits of those that we care about. We must form our own political coalitions. This is not a problem that has its solutions in liberalism, conservatism, democrats, republicans or any of that other nonsense that they feed you every day while trying to indoctrinate you into their way of thinking. It has to do with the fact that there is nothing wrong with being apologetically and genuinely black 100 percent of the time. You must seize your moment and NOT be afraid of who you really are.

You are the future. You are the visionary for your great-grandchildren. You are the one who's going to set the record straight and make sure that when people look back on the early 2000s, they realize that the future was set and determined by seeds that were planted by visionary black people like us. You are the runaway slave. You are the pioneer. You are the genius behind the movement that will take place within your own family.

The reason that you're reading this right now is because you are different. I am here to tell you that you are SUPPOSED to be different. God put you on this earth for a reason and it wasn't so that you could follow the crowd. It was so that you could LEAD the crowd. In order for us to move forward as a people, as a community, we must adopt a new paradigm of thinking, a new approach to solving problems, a new set of solutions and strategies that will elevate our people to the levels that we want them to go. We must apply these ideas relentlessly, fearlessly, and without worrying about who might object to what we choose to do.

I would like for you to read this document every time the world gets you down. Read it every time you are afraid. Glance at it every time you feel like what you are doing is hopeless. I want you to hold onto this, and I want you to believe in these ideas, because the future belongs to you.

It's time for a New Paradigm in Black America, and it all starts with what we do RIGHT NOW.